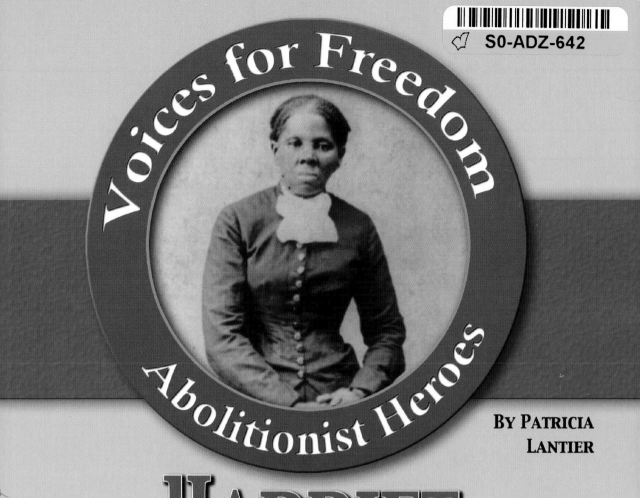

Voices for Freedom

Abolitionist Heroes

BY PATRICIA
LANTIER

HARRIET TUBMAN

Conductor on the Underground Railroad

CRABTREE
Publishing Company
www.crabtreebooks.com

Author: Patricia Lantier
Editors: Mark Sachner, Lynn Peppas
Publishing plan research and development:
    Sean Charlebois, Reagan Miller
    Crabtree Publishing Company
Proofreader: Ellen Rodger
Editorial director: Kathy Middleton
Photo research: Ruth Owen
Designer: Westgrapix/Tammy West
Production coordinator: Margaret Amy Salter
Production: Kim Richardson
Curriculum adviser: Suzy Gazlay, M.A.
Editorial consultant: James Marten, Ph.D.; Chair, Department
    of History, Marquette University, Milwaukee, Wisconsin

Front cover (inset), back cover, and title page: Photograph of
Harriet Tubman.
Front cover (bottom): A series of anti-slavery trading cards from
the 1800s, by American artist Henry Louis Stephens. Pictures like
this were used by abolitionists to convince people that slavery
should be stopped.

Written, developed, and produced by Water Buffalo Books

Photographs and reproductions:
Corbis: Vaningen-Snyder: page 8; Louie Psihoyos: page 10; page
19; pages 22-23 (center); C.H. Reed: page 38; page 47. Courtesy of
the Library of Congress: Image 3a10453: page 1; page 3; page 4
(top left); Image 3a18408: page 5 (top); Image 3a10453: page 12
(top left); Image 3c15201: page 13 (top); Image 007745: page 14
(left); Image LC-USZC4-5251: page 16; Image NW0151: page 20;
Image 3a10453: page 22 (top left); Image 3g02525: page 24 (right);
Image 3g02526: page 24 (left); Image 3g02521: page 31 (bottom);
Image 3a10453: page 32 (top left); page 32 (left); Image 3g04659:
page 33 (top); Image 3a06486: page 44; Image 3c12169: page 46;
Image 3g02519: page 48 (bottom); Image 19391: page 50 (top);
Image 3a24786: page 50 (bottom); Image 3a10453: page 51 (top
left); Image 02909: page 54. Galen Frysinger: page 7; page 40.
Getty Images: page 18; page 25; page 26; page 33 (bottom); Jerry
Pinkney: page 34; page 48 (top); Don Cravens: page 57. The
Granger Collection: page 11; page 27; page 55. NASA: page 9. The
New York Public Library: page 58. North Wind Picture Archives:
page 15; page 21. Shutterstock: pages 12-13 (background); page 14
(right); page 17; pages 30-31 (center); page 39; page 43. Superstock:
pages 4-5 (center); page 28; page 36 (left); page 51 (bottom).
WestGraphix: page 37. Wikipedia (public domain): page 6; page 29
(top right); page 29 (center left); page 35; page 41; page 53.

Library and Archives Canada Cataloguing in Publication

Lantier, Patricia, 1952-
    Harriet Tubman : conductor on the Underground
Railroad / Patricia Lantier.

(Voices for freedom: abolitionist heros)
Includes index.
ISBN 978-0-7787-4822-9 (bound).--ISBN 978-0-7787-4838-0 (pbk.)

    1. Tubman, Harriet, 1820?-1913--Juvenile literature.
2. Slaves--United States--Biography--Juvenile literature.
3. African American women--Biography--Juvenile literature.
4. Underground Railroad--Juvenile literature. I. Title.
II. Series: Voices for freedom: abolitionist heros

E444.T897L35 2009   j973.7'115092   C2009-903734-3

The Library of Congress has cataloged the printed edition as follows:

Lantier, Patricia, 1952-
 Harriet Tubman : conductor on the Underground Railroad /
Patricia Lantier.
    p. cm. -- (Voices for freedom. Abolitionist heros)
 Includes index.
 ISBN 978-0-7787-4838-0 (pbk. : alk. paper) -- ISBN 978-0-7787-4822-9
(reinforced library binding : alk. paper)
1. Tubman, Harriet, 1820?-1913--Juvenile literature. 2. Slaves--
United States--Biography--Juvenile literature. 3. African American
women--Biography--Juvenile literature. 4. Underground
Railroad--Juvenile literature. I. Title.
E444.T82L36 2010
973.7'115092--dc22
[B]
                                        2009023633

Crabtree Publishing Company

www.crabtreebooks.com   1-800-387-7650

Printed in the U.S.A./012014/SN20131105

**Published
in Canada
Crabtree Publishing**
616 Welland Ave.
St. Catharines, Ontario
L2M 5V6

**Published in
the United States
Crabtree Publishing**
PMB 59051
350 Fifth Ave., 59th Floor
New York, NY 10118

**Published in the
United Kingdom
Crabtree Publishing**
Maritime House
Basin Road North, Hove
BN41 1WR

**Published
in Australia
Crabtree Publishing**
3 Charles Street
Coburg North
VIC, 3058

Contents

CHAPTER ONE

Follow the North Star!

Harriet Tubman ran swiftly into the dark night. She was alone, without a path to travel through the dense terrain. She moved as quietly as possible, away from the main road. Harriet's master would soon realize she was missing and send the overseer with dogs and guns to look for her. Independent patrollers might also be on the lookout for a runaway.

Harriet Tubman, an escaped slave from Maryland, became an abolitionist, military spy, and women's activist. This statue in the South End of Boston honors Tubman in her role as emancipator of slaves. Working under the cloak of darkness, she led dozens of slaves out of captivity. During the Civil War, in an act of stunning bravery and military leadership, Harriet guided an expedition of Union soldiers on a raid in South Carolina that freed more than 700 slaves.

Slave quarters at a plantation in Savannah, Georgia. In addition to working long hours in the fields to produce large crop yields, many slaves worked in small industrial operations on the plantation. If any time was still available, slaves also provided labor for other plantation owners.

Determined to Make the Dream Come True

Harriet's long skirt caught on brambles as she ran. She sometimes tripped on branches and other obstacles covering the dark ground. Her heart was pounding, and she could barely catch her breath. She worried a bit about the frequent "sleeping spells" that were a constant part of her life. If she suddenly fell into a deep sleep, she needed to be hidden from view. In spite of her precarious situation, Harriet would not let fear change her purpose. She was physically strong from years of hard labor in the fields. She also was determined to make her dream of freedom come true.

Fear of the Unknown

Two weeks earlier, Harriet had attempted to escape with two of her brothers, Ben and Henry. All three were working away from their home plantation. When their owner realized the slaves were missing, she posted a notice in the local paper offering money for their capture.

The brothers did not agree with Harriet about which direction to run. After several days, they were afraid of being caught. They were lost and wanted to go back. Because they had been hired out to work at another plantation, their absence had not been noticed right away, which would reduce the amount of time they had been missed. Also, they were hard workers and hoped that if they provided a believable explanation for their absence, the consequences would not be too severe. Harriet did not want to turn back. She argued with her brothers, but they forced her to return.

Ready for Freedom

Back at work, Harriet heard that her owner had plans to sell her. She decided to leave again. This time she would go alone. She wanted to be free, and no one would stop her. For 27 years, she had been a slave—"hired out," or rented, by her master to strangers. Hiring out meant extra money for slave owners, who sometimes did not have enough work for all their slaves. Harriet could no longer tolerate the physical threats and mistreatment she had faced over the years.

Many of the people Harriet had worked for since early childhood were cruel. They rarely provided enough food or clothing and expected her to work long days at intense labor. Some beat Harriet even when she had done nothing wrong. They simply wanted to remind her that she was

THREE HUNDRED DOLLARS REWARD.

RANAWAY from the subscriber on Monday the 17th ult., three negroes, named as follows: HARRY, aged about 19 years, has on one side of his neck a won, just under the ear, he is of a dark chestnut color, about 5 feet 8 or 9 inches hight; BEN, aged about 25 years, is very quick to speak when spoken to, he is of a chestnut color, about six feet high; MINTY, aged about 27 years, is of a chestnut color, fine looking, and about 5 feet high. One hundred dollars reward will be given for each of the above named negroes, if taken out of the State, and $50 each if taken in the State. They must be lodged in Baltimore, Easton or Cambridge Jail, in Maryland.

ELIZA ANN BRODESS.
Near Bucktown, Dorchester county, Md.
Oct. 3d, 1849.

The Delaware Gazette will please copy the above three weeks, and charge this office.

Eliza Brodess, widow of Edward Brodess, owned Harriet (Minty) and her brothers Henry (Harry) and Ben when they attempted to escape in 1849. Mrs. Brodess published this notice of reward in the *Cambridge Democrat.* The notice included the ages and physical descriptions of the runaways.

The Underground Railroad

As a child, Harriet Tubman sometimes heard other slaves speak in hushed voices about an Underground Railroad. This mysterious "railroad" provided a way for slaves to escape bondage and live free. Many slaves did not understand how a railroad could be underground. Were there secret tunnels that trains traveled through to go north?

This didn't seem likely, but no one was certain. When Harriet finally made her bid for freedom, she learned that the Underground Railroad was actually a secret network of people and safe houses that provided shelter, food, clothing, and transportation for runaway slaves as they made their way to free states or Canada.

Historians believe that most escaping slaves probably did not have the benefit of the Underground Railroad. It was particularly prominent in the region known as the Upper South, especially in states that bordered the North. Harriet's experience as a slave escaping from Maryland was probably more typical of that region than in the area known as the Lower South, or Deep South. There, in states such as Alabama, Georgia, South Carolina, Louisiana, and Mississippi, slave labor played a big part in the growing and harvesting of cotton. Escape from those states was even more difficult than in the Upper South.

Courageous participants in the Underground Railroad usually left a candle burning in a window of their houses at night. The candle served as a sign to runaway slaves that they could stop for food and shelter. This particular "safe house" is part of a display at the National Underground Railroad Freedom Center in Cincinnati, Ohio.

their property. She had a family she could visit now and then, but her being able to see them was determined by where they were working at any given time.

Many slaves were beaten frequently, either by their owners or by men called "overseers" who managed large numbers of plantation slaves. This engraving printed in 1864 shows some of the cruel punishments slaves had to endure. Often, other slaves were forced to gather and witness the beatings.

Life without freedom became unbearable for the young woman. Harriet wanted to escape farther north, to a free state, where she might have some chance at a life of her own.

Running away was very dangerous. Harriet could not take the risk of telling anyone that she was leaving again, especially after the recent incident with her brothers. She wanted to tell her mother, but she knew her mother's grief might draw attention. Unable to tell anyone directly about her plans, she managed to leave a message to friends at the plantation by singing a spiritual that carried a secret message.

Running for Her Life

As she made her way north, Harriet thought about those she loved and the life of bondage she was leaving behind. She had left everyone she knew, even her husband and other family members she could only see from time to time. She would have to depend on the help of strangers and her own courage in the days ahead. She could not look back or doubt her mission.

How could it be right to enslave people? To "own" anyone—to have the power to sell them and beat them and tear apart their families in order to make money—defied explanation. Harriet could not read or write. Many states had laws prohibiting the education of slaves. Slave owners believed

The Drinking Gourd

Many slaves knew the Big Dipper as the Drinking Gourd. The shape of this cluster of stars reminded them of a long-handled utensil, made from a hollowed gourd, that they used to collect and drink water. The slaves would study the gourd in the night sky, paying particular attention to the two stars at the edge of the "cup." These two stars point to Polaris, also known as the North Star. The North Star never moves in the sky. Runaway slaves had to travel north, toward a free state or Canada. Many would find the Drinking Gourd and locate the North Star. This helped them travel in the right direction.

A song titled "Follow the Drinking Gourd" was first published in 1928. Many people say this song is very old and carries a code of safe passage that was used by slaves as they made their way north. One version of the first verse is as follows:

> *When the sun comes back and the first quail calls,*
> *Follow the Drinking Gourd.*
> *For the old man is waiting for to carry you to freedom,*
> *If you follow the Drinking Gourd.*

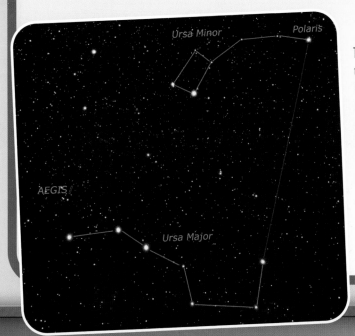

This map shows the seven stars that form the Big Dipper, also known to slaves as the Drinking Gourd. The two stars at the right edge of the cup point straight up to Polaris, or the North Star, which never moves in the sky. Polaris is also the ladle tip of the star cluster named the Little Dipper. Slaves on the run followed the North Star to freedom.

ignorance would keep the slaves close to home. Even without formal education, Harriet was smart and had common sense. She knew the difference between right and wrong. Slavery was wrong.

If captured and dragged back to the main plantation residence, or Big House, there was a chance that Harriet would be branded with an R (runaway), whipped in front of the other slaves, and sold to another slave owner who lived far away from Maryland. Her life could be even worse and more confining than before, and she would never see her family again. Harriet was not certain what would happen once she reached the free state of Pennsylvania but knew she could find a way to survive on her own. After saving her wages for a while, she would help her family reach

I had reasoned this out in my mind; there was one of two things I had a right to, liberty or death; if I could not have one, I would have the other."

— Harriet
Tubman

An early picture of Harriet Tubman. A burning candle, perhaps a symbol of safety and the light of freedom, sits on a Bible placed in front of the framed image in Harriet's home in Auburn, New York.

freedom, too. She would convince her husband to join her.

These thoughts gave Harriet the strength and will to keep moving quickly through the night. She watched her step as best she could and looked up toward what she had heard whispered in the slave cabins—to follow the North Star in the dark sky that would lead her to freedom.

Harriet also had great faith in God. She prayed as she ran and trusted that He would protect her. Harriet's strong faith gave her courage. She would succeed in this escape. Her life was at stake. Harriet would never be a slave again.

This portrait of Frederick Douglass shows the young man at about age 26, approximately six years after his escape from slavery. His first autobiography, *Narrative of the Life of Frederick Douglass: An American Slave*, was published in 1845, when he was 27.

Frederick Douglass and The North Star

Frederick Douglass was a plantation slave born in Maryland. His master sent him to relatives in Baltimore as a child. While there, he learned to read and write. Douglass made a bold escape from slavery as a young man. He worked as an abolitionist, even though he was still legally a slave. To avoid capture, Douglass traveled for two years in Europe, talking to interested audiences about the evils of slavery. He was a gifted speaker. In 1846, two friends in England purchased his freedom. Douglass returned to the United States and lived with his family in Rochester, New York. Their home was a safe house on the Underground Railroad. In 1847, Douglass began publishing an anti-slavery newspaper called *The North Star*. He named the paper after the bright star that guided slaves to freedom.

CHAPTER TWO

Growing Up in Slavery

Harriet Tubman's birth name was Araminta "Minty" Ross. She was born, probably in 1822, on a plantation owned by Anthony Thompson in Dorchester County, Maryland. Harriet's parents were Benjamin Ross and Harriet "Rit" Greene. Minty, who later changed her name to Harriet, was the fifth of nine children. Her parents were both slaves, but they did not have the same master. Anthony Thompson owned Ben Ross. Thompson's stepson, Edward Brodess, owned Harriet Greene. The Brodess plantation was also in Dorchester County.

Moving Around

Ben Ross lived and worked on the Thompson plantation unless he was hired out to do work for other landowners. Ben and Rit married around 1808 and lived together on Thompson land until 1824. That year, young

Slaves labor in a plantation cotton field. Conditions for field hands were harsh. Slaves most often picked cotton with their bare hands in blistering heat from sunrise to sundown six days a week, with little food and water.

Edward Brodess inherited his mother's estate. He received land and slaves that had belonged to his mother's family, including Rit and her children. Rit moved with her family to work on the Brodess property.

Child Labor

Edward Brodess began hiring Harriet out to other landowners when she was just six years old. Many masters treated her badly. Severe beatings quickly became part of her life. Her first hire was to a farmer named James Cook. Mrs. Cook wanted help with her weaving. Young Harriet stood for long hours winding yarn each day. Most of the time, she was cold and hungry. She did not learn weaving very well.

The small cabin Harriet lived in with her family as a young child may have been similar to this cabin on the Womack-Crenshaw Plantation in Alabama.

In direct contrast to the small, cramped cabins in the slave quarters, the main house on a plantation was often large and grand. Several slaves worked at the "Big House" as housekeepers, personal maids, nannies, cooks, laundresses, gardeners, groundskeepers, and other positions that supported the rituals of daily life.

Mr. Cook forced Harriet to trap muskrats. She worked outdoors in the cold and damp, wading through marshy land and nearby streams. She developed a serious case of measles and bronchitis but continued working. She became so ill that she returned to the Brodess plantation to recover.

After several weeks, Harriet returned to the Cook home. She disliked being in the small house and did not want to weave. Mrs. Cook finally sent Harriet back to Edward Brodess for good, saying she was of no help and could not learn.

Nowhere to Hide

Harriet worked next for a married woman named Miss Susan. Susan hired the young girl to be a nursemaid to her baby. She also expected Harriet to do housework. Harriet did not know how to clean house. No one had taught her. Susan beat Harriet repeatedly for not cleaning the house properly.

Nat Turner's Rebellion

As a girl, Harriet Tubman heard the dramatic story of Nat Turner. Turner was a slave in Virginia who led a rebellion. He was a religious man who had learned to read and write. He worked as a preacher when not laboring in the fields, and became known as "The Prophet."

In 1831, Nat Turner had a vision calling him to action, saying he was to "slay [his] enemies with their own weapons." In August of that year, Nat and four other slaves rebelled against their servitude. They killed their master and his family, then went on to kill more than 50 other white people in 24 hours. Turner and his growing band of followers freed all slaves along the way. The rebel group was stopped within 48 hours, but Turner managed to elude capture until October. He was tried and hanged for his offenses.

During the year or two after the Nat Turner rebellion, there was a huge crackdown against unruly slaves in Virginia and North Carolina. Dozens of Turner's followers were killed or punished. Some historians have estimated that even more slaves not associated with the rebellion were killed or punished for suspicious behavior. Still, the life and death of Nat Turner marked a change in the relationship between slaves and their owners. The rebellion was a sign to all involved that freedom might not be a hopeless dream forever.

Nat Turner's violent rebellion against slavery did not last long, but it made a deep impression on slaves and slave owners alike. Turner hid in the countryside and managed to elude capture for about two months. Before his hanging, he told his story to a lawyer named Thomas R. Gray, who later published "The Confessions of Nat Turner" in several newspapers.

This image of a white child held by her slave nursemaid could serve as a mirror of Harriet's relationship with Miss Susan's child. Although house servants had a higher status than slaves who worked in the fields, the photographer here chose to remind those who looked at the photo that the main subject was the baby, not the slave. The nursemaid's face is partially hidden; she is simply part of the background. It is the child, with her hand-colored face and dress, who stands out and attracts attention.

After long days of tending the baby and keeping the house in order, Harriet had to rock the baby through the night. Her mistress did not want to be disturbed. If Harriet fell asleep from exhaustion, and the baby woke up and cried, Miss Susan would grab the nearby whip and beat Harriet again.

One day, Miss Susan and her husband had a loud argument in the kitchen. Harriet was in the room and took a small piece of sugar from a bowl on the table. Susan saw Harriet take the sugar and immediately reached for the whip. Harriet ran from the house until she reached a farm a good distance away. She climbed into a pigpen and stayed there for several days, fighting for food scraps.

Harriet knew she had to return to Miss Susan's house. As she later explained, "I was so starved I had to go back to my Missus, I hadn't got no where else to go, but I knowed what was coming."

Miss Susan tried to whip Harriet when she returned, but Harriet would not let her. Later, the master came home and beat Harriet so hard he broke her ribs and caused other internal injuries. Unable to work, Harriet returned to the Brodess homestead. The beatings she received during her time at Miss Susan's house left scars that never went away.

A Wound to Last a Lifetime

As a young teenager, Harriet was hired out to a neighboring plantation. She worked in the fields. One day, she walked with the house cook to a

At this time, fresh produce and goods such as flour and sugar did not come pre-packaged but were sold loose in whatever quantity the customer needed. The goods would be weighed using scales and heavy lead or brass weights. It was one such weight that hit Harriet in the forehead, causing headaches and other medical problems that affected her for her entire life.

local general store to purchase supplies. She noticed a male slave running away. An overseer followed close behind. Both men ran into the store. Harriet went up the steps as the slave was running back toward the door to get out again.

The overseer yelled at Harriet to block the passage. Harriet let the slave out, then stood in the doorway. The angry overseer grabbed a two-pound (one-kilogram) weight from a counter and threw it with all his strength toward the runaway. He missed the male slave but hit Harriet right in the middle of her forehead, so hard that it broke her skull.

Severely wounded, Harriet was taken back to the house. In her words: "They carried me to the house all bleeding and fainting. I had no bed, no place to lie down on at all, and they lay me on the seat of the loom, and I stayed there all that day and next, and the next day I went to work again and there I worked with the blood and sweat rolling down my face till I couldn't see." Harriet was sent back to the Brodess plantation.

During the long, painful months of recovery that followed, Edward Brodess tried to sell Harriet. No one was interested in purchasing such a disabled slave. The terrible injury had lifelong consequences. In addition to a large scar on her forehead, Harriet experienced severe headaches and unusual "sleeping spells." Without warning, she would fall into a deep sleep, during which she could not be awakened. These episodes varied in length, from several minutes to more than an hour. After a while, she would awaken on her own and continue with what she had been doing or saying before falling asleep. Harriet also began having prophetic dreams, nightmares, and visions. She believed these visions were signs from God to help guide her through life.

Modern medical knowledge indicates that Harriet's sleeping spells may have been seizures. The "spells" occurred frequently throughout the rest of Harriet's life.

Rebuilding Strength

In 1836, when she was a teenager, Harriet was hired out to John T. Stewart. Stewart's family owned a large farm, general store, shipyard, and lumber business. At first, Harriet worked as a house servant. Later, she asked her master if she could work outdoors. Although she was not very

A white landowner in Texas keeps an eye on the slaves picking cotton on his plantation. Many wealthy landowners used overseers to manage the large slave labor force required to keep the plantation in smooth working order.

Overseers and Drivers

Large plantations needed the work of many slaves to remain prosperous. Some slaves worked at the main plantation house. Others tended gardens, maintained the grounds, and cared for the livestock. Most, however, toiled long days in the fields.

Many slave owners employed overseers and drivers. These men worked as supervisors. Drivers usually were slaves who had demonstrated an ability to lead others. They most often worked as assistants to white overseers, especially on the larger plantations. On smaller farms, some drivers managed the slaves on their own.

Profit at any cost was the landowners' goal. This meant overseers and drivers had the power to discipline slaves in any way that would make them docile yet highly productive.

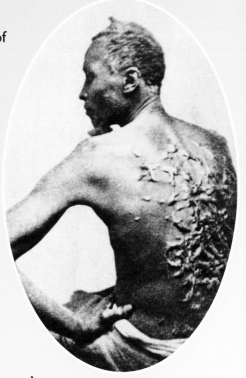

In an 1863 photo, a freed slave named Gordon, from Louisiana, shows the deep network of scars he received from repeated whippings.

tall, John Stewart knew that she was physically very strong. He had seen her lifting large barrels and hauling heavy loads to and from the buildings on his property.

Stewart agreed to let Harriet work outdoors. She worked in the fields and cut lumber in the forests. She did all the work a man was expected to do. Stewart was impressed with Harriet's hard work and strength. He would often make Harriet show visitors how strong she was when they came to visit. One of the feats that he had her perform to impress his friends was having her use ropes to pull a barge along the river on his property.

In the 1840s, Harriet returned to the Brodess plantation. She received permission to hire herself out to other landowners in the area. This was a privilege usually granted only to trusted slaves. The arrangement was good for both Harriet and Brodess. Harriet was Brodess's property. She had to pay him a good part of what she earned. She could keep the rest. Harriet bought her own team of oxen. Now in her 20s, Harriet worked as much as she could on outside jobs, using the oxen to help ready fields for farming by clearing the land of timber and hauling the lumber away.

Marriage and a New Name

In 1844, Harriet married a free black man named John Tubman. John was the son of free parents. Many black people in the United States had never been slaves. Others were slaves who bought their freedom after years of hard work. Some slaves were granted freedom when their masters died. Other slave owners would manumit, or free, their slaves after they had worked a certain number of years.

As a free man, John could move where he chose. Harriet, however, had to remain close in Dorchester County. She was hiring herself out during this time, so the couple may have been able to live together—or near each other.

Although cotton was the main cash crop on wealthy plantations in the South, several other crops were profitable, too. In this photograph from the early 1860s, workers in South Carolina are tending a sweet potato field.

Jumping the Broom

Marriage between slaves was not legally recognized. Owners could always sell one or both partners at any time. For this reason, most wedding ceremonies were informal.

Sometimes, two slaves received permission to marry from their master (or masters) and simply moved into the same cabin. Others had to live apart and struggle to find a way to see each other. One ceremony that offered slaves an opportunity to publicly pledge their commitment to each other was called "jumping the broom." This ceremony usually took place in the presence of other members of the slave community.

The custom of jumping the broom varied slightly from place to place. Sometimes, the bride and groom held hands and jumped together to the sound of beating drums over brooms placed on the ground. Another approach was to have each partner jump separately over a broom held about a foot off the ground. If either missed the jump, the other would rule the household. If both partners cleared the jump, they would be equal decision makers.

Members of a slave community gather in their best clothes to witness, show support, and celebrate a broomstick wedding ceremony.

CHAPTER THREE

Flight to Freedom

Over the years, Edward Brodess had sold Harriet's three older sisters, either to pay debts or purchase land. Harriet had nightmares about being sold. She did not want to be separated forever from her husband and the rest of her family.

Edward Brodess died in 1849. His wife Eliza soon made plans to sell part of the family land and several slaves to pay her husband's substantial debts. Harriet's fears were closer to coming true. She heard rumors that she would be sold. She talked to John Tubman about running away. She tried to enlist his support. John told Harriet to stop talking about escape. He would not help her.

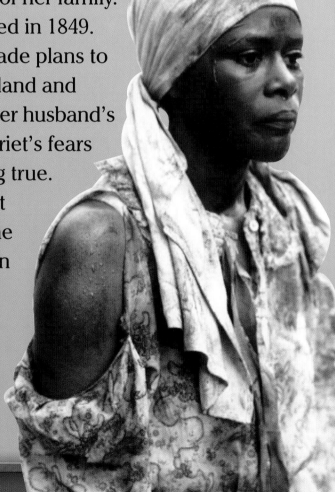

Ready to Strike Out on Her Own

John Tubman did not like Harriet's dreams and visions. He did not even want to hear about them. He said they were proof she was dull-witted and could not think clearly.

Harriet did not want to wait to be sold. One nightmare in particular occurred frequently. She dreamed of men on horses storming into the slave quarters. Women and children screamed as they were forcibly separated and taken away. Harriet would awaken from these dreams crying, "Oh, they're coming, they're coming, I must go."

A First Attempt

In September 1849, Harriet ran away with two of her brothers, Ben and Henry. They all worked on or near the Thompson plantation at that time. They knew Mistress Eliza Brodess had difficulty running the family plantation after her husband's death. Keeping track of her slaves was a big problem because many were hired out. Word of the siblings' disappearance might not reach her for some time.

Two weeks later, Eliza Brodess suspected the three had run away. She posted a notice that described the physical appearance of Harriet and her brothers. She offered a reward for their capture and return.

Facing page: Cicely Tyson plays the role of Harriet Tubman in a movie titled *A Woman Called Moses*. This moving drama tells the story of Harriet's amazing and inspiring life. Her fight for freedom from slavery as well as her work as conductor on the Underground Railroad, Civil War spy, and political activist all come together in this remarkable epic.

Ben and Henry were tired and frightened. They decided to return to the Thompson plantation. Both were willing to take their chances with Master Thompson and Eliza Brodess. Harriet wanted to continue on her own, but Ben and Henry brought her back with them.

THE SALE.

THE PARTING "Buy us too."

Although slaves were encouraged to "marry" and have children, their masters had the right to sell one or more family members at any time. Most slaves worried constantly about being separated from their loved ones forever. Without warning, a father, mother, or child could be taken from the slave quarter and brought to auction. These illustrations by American artist Henry Louis Stephens depict the trauma of tearing families apart at auction time.

Bound for the Promised Land

The slaves were always on the lookout for any kind of news they could gather concerning what fate—and their masters—held in store for them. Two days after Harriet had returned to the plantation, rumors that she had been sold followed her everywhere. Harriet knew she had to run away again.

Harriet was not certain how to leave word about her plans. She decided to confide in a friend named Mary. Mary worked in the Big House and was trustworthy, but Harriet could not find a way to be alone with her friend. She finally began to walk toward the house. She would sing a spiritual, a religious song, with words that described leaving for the Promised Land. This way, Mary would hear Harriet and know her friend was bound for freedom.

Harriet had a beautiful, distinctive voice. She had grown up attending religious services on Sundays. She could not read, but she knew stories

Grandmother Modesty

Harriet Tubman's maternal grandmother's name was Modesty. She may have been taken as a child from Africa's Gold Coast region and shipped as a slave to the North American colonies.

Harriet believed she was descended from the Ashanti (Asante) people through her grandmother. The Ashanti were from the area of Africa now known as Ghana. Harriet heard about this ancestry as a child. Ashanti slaves were valuable because of their physical strength and their ability to do many types of work. These proud people were also fiercely independent.

A wealthy man named Atthow Pattison was Edward Brodess's great grandfather. Pattison owned land and slaves in Maryland in the 1700s. Modesty was a slave on the Pattison plantation. Her daughter "Rit" was Harriet's mother. Atthow Pattison gave Rit to his granddaughter Mary as a personal slave. Mary later married Joseph Brodess. Together they had a son named Edward. When Edward Brodess became old enough to own property, he inherited land and slaves, including Rit and her children. Harriet (Araminta), daughter of Rit and granddaughter of Modesty, belonged to Edward Brodess.

During the years of American slavery, native Africans were often sold as soon as the ships carrying them landed on American soil. This engraving shows a Dutch ship in the early 1600s recently arrived with a group of slaves for sale in Jamestown, Virginia.

from the Bible and sang spirituals with her family and the community of slaves and free black people in the area. Harriet had a deep faith and trust in God and knew He would help her at this time. She began to sing:

I'm sorry I'm going to leave you,
    Farewell, oh farewell;
But I'll meet you in the morning,
    Farewell, oh farewell.

I'll meet you in the morning,
I'm bound for the promised land,
On the other side of Jordan,
Bound for the promised land.

Having left a message for the people she cared most about, Harriet ran away that night, moving as swiftly as she could and staying well hidden. She knew her way through part of the woods. She had labored in the area for many years for John Stewart. She managed to make her way through that first night without encountering anyone. In order to stay in the right direction, she followed the light of the North Star that shone dimly through the cloudy sky.

Plantation slaves worked long hours during the day and had little personal time. Sundays were the exception on some plantations. On that day, slaves were allowed to attend church services and have a few hours of free time to spend with their friends and families. Harriet enjoyed going to church on Sundays. She liked singing spirituals and listening to the sermons. She also enjoyed the close feeling of community when the people around her spent free time together.

Slaves who ran away were at great risk of being captured and dragged back to their owners. Some masters sent their overseers or an armed posse to track the slaves. Others counted on the activities of patrollers who spent their time searching for escaped slaves in exchange for a monetary reward. This image shows a runaway who has been "treed" by search dogs and mounted slave hunters.

Help from Kind Strangers

The first stop at the end of the night was a home that had been described to Harriet as a safe house. She carried a piece of paper with two names on it. A woman who lived near the Thompson plantation had offered more than once to help Harriet if she ever decided to leave. It was this woman who had written the names down and explained to Harriet where to stop.

Harriet had great courage. When she reached the house, she knocked on the door. A woman opened it. After seeing the piece of paper, she gave Harriet food to eat. She then told Harriet to sweep the steps and yard. This would make anyone who had seen Harriet believe she had come to work. That night, the woman's husband hid Harriet in a covered wagon. He drove her a good distance away.

Harriet continued to travel in this fashion. She walked mostly at night in order to avoid capture. The people at whose homes she stopped gave her food, shelter, and rest. Some were able to provide transportation for a small distance. Each gave her the name and directions of another place to stop. When traveling alone, Harriet glanced up at the night sky to maintain her northbound progress.

The Underground Railroad that Harriet had heard whispered about was working. Many people in the United States did not believe in slavery.

Slaves who had the courage to try to escape their lives of bondage often faced hazardous traveling conditions. Nights were longer in winter, so most ran away in the cold months. This gave them more time to travel under the cover of darkness. The weather was often brutal, as shown in this painting by artist Charles T. Webber. Many runaways, worried about capture, and traveling for days without sufficient food or warm clothing, wondered if they had made the right decision.

They knew it was morally wrong and wanted to abolish the institution. These people were called "abolitionists."

Abolitionists who worked as members of the Underground Railroad included both black and white people. They tried to help slaves reach freedom farther north, either in the United States or in Canada. They offered their homes as places to hide runaways for a short time. They did this work as secretly as possible so the slaves would not be discovered. Also, abolitionists who opened their homes could get into trouble for their activities. It was illegal to harbor fugitive slaves.

On her journey, Harriet had to trust people she had never met. She was amazed at the kindness of those who would help strangers even while placing themselves in danger. Traveling alone through unfamiliar land was difficult, but Harriet kept heading north, talking and praying to God to help her find the way to the next safe place.

Quakers and Abolition

Quakers are members of The Society of Friends, a religious group founded in England in the 1600s. Followers are also known as Friends. The Quaker community spread to other parts of the world, including the United States. Members believe in peace. They do not support war. They also believe in integrity, simplicity, the possibility of direct communication with God, and the equality of all people. Many Quakers had opposed slavery as individuals from the time of the group's founding. In the 1700s, especially around the time of the American Revolution in the mid-to-late 1700s, the group as a whole emerged as abolitionist.

During the time of slavery in the United States, many Quakers played a significant role in assisting runaway slaves. Two major Quaker abolitionists during this time were Levi Coffin and his wife Catharine. Their home was a safe house on the Railroad and sometimes referred to as "Grand Central Station." Some historians estimate that the couple harbored and helped more than 2,000 slaves.

Originally from South Carolina, Quaker abolitionists Levi (above right) and Catharine Coffin moved to Indiana and offered their home as a safe house to runaway slaves for 20 years. Slaves who were able to make their way to the Coffin house could hide in a small, secret room in an upstairs bedroom whose door was hidden by a tall headboard. Levi Coffin was often referred to as the "president of the Underground Railroad."

The Dream Comes True

The closest free state to Maryland was Pennsylvania. Harriet's destination was the city of Philadelphia. Many fugitive slaves had found a certain measure of freedom there. To reach the Pennsylvania state line, Harriet had to travel through areas of her native Maryland as well as the northeastern section of the state of Delaware. The distance was about 90 miles (145 kilometers). She would then make her way to Philadelphia.

Harriet never doubted that her path was the right one. She wanted freedom and was willing to sacrifice everything. She had decided that

"...no man should take me alive; I should fight for my liberty as long as my strength lasted, and when the time came for me to go, the Lord would let them take me."

After many days of traveling and hiding, Harriet approached the state line from Delaware into Pennsylvania. She would soon cross from slavery into freedom. She was a fugitive, so the possibility of capture would follow her. Still, a freedom Harriet had never experienced before would be hers.

Harriet remembered a recurring dream she had before her escape. In this dream, Harriet was flying over large areas of unfamiliar landscapes.

After many miles, she reached a river she needed to cross. She did not think she had enough strength left. Harriet fell toward the water. Before sinking into the river, a group of ladies dressed in white reached their arms out to her and pulled her across to safety.

Harriet realized as she traveled north that the landscapes she crossed were the same as those in the dream. Many of the ladies who helped her along the way looked like those she had seen in the dream. One obvious similarity was that they were white, but she also believed that the women wore the same white clothing and resembled those she had seen in her dreams. These similarities had a profound effect on her as traveled north.

Harriet finally crossed the state line. She was overwhelmed by her escape to Pennsylvania and also by the idea that she was free:

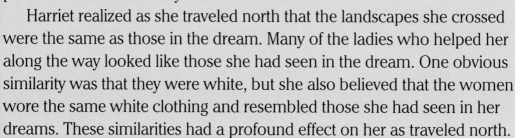

When I found I had crossed that line, I looked at my hands to see if I was the same person. There was such a glory over everything; the sun came like gold through the trees, and over the fields, and I felt like I was in heaven.

Above: A beautiful woodland creek, such as this one in Maryland, may have presented one of the many physical challenges runaway slaves encountered on their journey to freedom. Keeping off the main roads and pathways meant traveling in darkness through unfamiliar terrain with unexpected obstacles.

Right: In this illustration by American artist Henry Louis Stephens, a slave shows his intense feelings of joy at having reached freedom. As Harriet expressed when she crossed the state line into Pennsylvania, being free felt like "heaven."

Fearless Conductor on the Underground Railroad

CHAPTER FOUR

Overwhelmed by the size and bustle of Philadelphia, Harriet realized freedom had yet another price. She was lonely. She missed her family and friends. As she later explained, "There was no one to welcome me to the land of freedom. I was a stranger in a strange land; and my home, after all, was down in Maryland; because my father, my mother, my brothers and sister and friends were there."

A Renewed Sense of Purpose

Harriet decided that her real mission in life had just begun. She would work to bring all her family to freedom.

A classic and often-reproduced portrait of Harriet taken by photographer H. B. Lindsley. Some sources estimate this photo was taken sometime in the 1860s, when Harriet would have been in her 40s.

Henry Brown was born a slave in Virginia in 1815. Separated from his family in 1830 to work in a tobacco factory, he married a few years later, and the couple had at least three children. Brown's wife and children were sold in 1848 and sent to North Carolina. Heartbroken, Brown determined to escape slavery. He found a white shoemaker who agreed to ship him in a crate from Richmond, Virginia, to the office of the Pennsylvania Anti-Slavery Society in Philadelphia. In this illustration, Henry "Box" Brown emerges from the crate as several figures, including Frederick Douglass, watch in surprise. Details of Brown's escape were published in an autobiography titled *The Narrative of Henry Box Brown* in 1849.

"I was free, and they should be free."

With a renewed sense of purpose, she quickly found work as a house servant and hotel cook. She also found an inexpensive place to live. She saved her wages to rescue her loved ones.

Early in 1850, Harriet met black abolitionist William Still. Still was a leading figure in the Underground Railroad. He worked for the Philadelphia Vigilance Committee and was an active member of the Pennsylvania Anti-Slavery Society. Harriet began attending Vigilance Committee meetings. Members helped runaway slaves arriving in the city. She and Still became friends and colleagues.

William Still (1821–1902) was an African-American abolitionist and historian who worked for the Philadelphia Anti-Slavery Society. Still kept detailed records of the runaway slaves who came through the Philadelphia office. He was also the author of *The Underground Railroad*, probably the most complete existing record of the Railroad. The book also recorded the abolitionist movement and listed fugitives who began new lives with help from abolitionists.

Harriet led runaway slaves to Philadelphia when she first began her work as a conductor on the Underground Railroad. Fugitives were generally safe in the city, even though they were still technically slaves. With the passing of the Fugitive Slave Act of 1850, Harriet knew the only safe place for runaways was outside the United States. She began leading people to Canada. In this illustration by American artist Jerry Pinkney, Harriet is the woman dressed in blue.

The Mission Begins

In December 1850, Harriet organized her first trip back to Maryland. She had heard that her niece Kessiah, as well as Kessiah's two children, would be sold at auction. The Vigilance Committee and a brother-in-law in Baltimore offered their support. Harriet devised a plan to rescue her niece at the auction house. The risky mission was successful. Harriet met Kessiah and her family in Baltimore and led them safely to Philadelphia. A few months later, Harriet returned to Baltimore, this time to lead her brother Moses and two other slaves to freedom. This trip was risky, but Harriet managed to get herself and her companions through it safe and sound. Greater risks lay ahead.

Moving Past Her Sadness

Harriet's next trip was to Dorchester County, Maryland. She had to return to her former home. She would find John Tubman and convince him to move with her to Pennsylvania. The couple had not seen each other for two years. John answered her knock at their cabin door. When Harriet told him why she had returned, John told her that he had married again. He would not be going to Philadelphia.

With a heavy heart, Harriet turned away from her husband. She had to continue without him. She found a group of slaves who wanted freedom and brought them back with her.

The Fugitive Slave Act

Fugitive slaves had a certain amount of liberty and stability in the free states. A vague threat of being reclaimed was always present but didn't happen very often. A law that already existed allowed federal agents to hunt down anyone accused of being a runaway slave and force him or her back into slavery. In 1850, the U.S. Congress passed the Fugitive Slave Act, which dramatically changed this situation. The Act, passed in part to satisfy lawmakers from the South who wanted stronger federal laws to make it more difficult to help escaped slaves, did just that—it reinforced the earlier law stating that all runaway slaves had to be returned to their owners.

Many states had previously passed their own laws stating that their residents were not required to help federal officials find fugitive slaves. The new law basically forced state officials to aid federal marshals and judges when slave owners came looking for fugitives. Those who helped slaves escape would suffer harsh consequences.

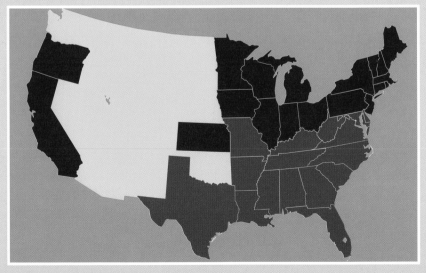

A map of the United States from 1861 shows the free states, slave states, and territories that had not yet been divided into states. The slave states are depicted in red and the free states in blue. When the Confederacy was formed, four slave states remained in the Union—Missouri, Kentucky, Maryland, and Delaware.

300 DOLLARS REWARD!

RUNAWAY from John S. Doak on the 21st inst., two NEGRO MEN; LOGAN 45 years of age, bald-headed, one or more crooked fingers; DAN 21 years old, six feet high. Both black. I will pay ONE HUNDRED DOLLARS for the apprehension and delivery of LOGAN, or to have him confined so that I can get him. I will also pay TWO HUNDRED DOLLARS for the apprehension of DAN, or to have him confined so that I can get him.
JOHN S. DOAKE,
Springfield, Mo., April 24th, 1857,

This 1857 poster from slave owner John S. Doake of Missouri offers a $300 reward for two male slave runaways. As with most posters of this kind, a description of each fugitive is provided to help locate the "property."

The new law was controversial. Many abolitionists and anti-slavery sympathizers spoke out fiercely against it. Some refused to follow the law. Harriet decided Canada would be the final destination on future trips north with runaways. She would take them to St. Catharines, Ontario, just over the border.

Elusive Moses

Gaining a reputation as a fearless conductor on the Underground Railroad, Harriet returned several times to Maryland. She led more family members and other slaves to freedom. The groups traveled by night. They often found food and temporary shelter at the homes of anti-slavery sympathizers in the region. Slave owners began to hear about someone called "Moses," who was leading slaves to freedom. They never suspected it was a woman.

Harriet's mission to lead others to freedom was unusual. Most slaves who managed to reach free states remained there. They dared not reenter slave states. Harriet possessed rare courage, a belief in her dreams and visions, and a deep faith in God. As a conductor, she risked not only her freedom, but also her life.

Harriet became successful at disguises, even though they were quite ordinary. Sometimes she dressed as a man. Other times, she wore loose-fitting clothes and large bonnets that covered her face. She often pretended to be elderly and walked bent over or with a cane in public. She learned how to avoid attention as she made her way through slave territory.

"Go Down, Moses"

In the Bible, Moses was a Hebrew child rescued from a river and raised by an Egyptian pharaoh's daughter. The daughter did not know Moses was a Hebrew. At that time, Hebrews in Egypt were slaves.

As a young man, Moses killed an Egyptian man in order to save a Hebrew slave. He was banished from Egypt. According to the Bible, God appeared to Moses in the desert and commanded him to lead the Hebrews out of bondage. Moses returned to Egypt and gathered his people. He led them through the desert and across the Red Sea toward the Promised Land of Canaan. This journey to freedom was called the Exodus, and the part of the Bible that records the story is called the Book of Exodus.

Like Moses, Harriet Tubman was born a slave. Also like Moses, she led many slaves away from bondage to a land of freedom. For this reason, many called Harriet the "Moses" of her people. Harriet often sang a spiritual titled "Go Down, Moses." The first verses are as follows:

> *When Israel was in Egypt's land,*
> *Let my people go.*
> *Oppressed so hard they could not stand,*
> *Let my people go.*
>
> *Go down, Moses,*
> *Way down in Egypt's land.*
> *Tell ole Pharaoh,*
> *Let my people go.*

In the biblical story of the Exodus, Moses led the Hebrew slaves out of Egypt and presented them with the rules that all followers of God must follow. These rules, which were carved on two stone tablets, are known as the Ten Commandments.

Fierce Leader

Slaves who left with Harriet were not allowed to change their minds. Harriet carried a firearm on each trip for defense purposes. If necessary, she would also use it to convince frightened slaves to remain with the group. She knew that if runaways were captured, they could be tortured into giving details about the other escapees, the routes Harriet used, or her identity. Her response to those who wanted to turn back was, "Go on or die!" Although there is no record of her having used her weapon against runaway slaves, she was clearly prepared to use force to protect the mission and the safety of the other runaways.

In 1854, Harriet planned the escape of her brothers Robert, Ben, and Henry. She arrived in Dorchester County on Christmas Eve and met her brothers near their father's cabin. Three other slave friends joined the group. Harriet sent two of the friends to alert her father. They urged Old Ben not to tell Rit. She would insist on seeing her children and be in danger as a witness.

Old Ben brought food to the hiding place and spoke to his children. Before leaving that night, Harriet and her brothers crept close to the cabin and looked inside to see Rit. Harriet had not seen her mother for several years.

An engraving that appears in William Still's book *The Underground Railroad* shows fugitive slaves defending themselves against patrollers or other slave catchers who wanted a hefty monetary reward. These slaves traveled in a covered wagon as they made their way to freedom.

St. Catharines

St. Catharines in Canada was the final stop for hundreds of slaves making their way to freedom from the United States. The city is located in the Niagara region of Ontario. The people of St. Catharines played an important role in the work of the Underground Railroad. The large abolitionist population there helped provide a safe haven for escaped slaves.

The 1850 Fugitive Slave Law in the United States meant runaway slaves had to leave their country in order to find freedom. Harriet Tubman brought her family and other fugitives to St. Catharines. She made her home in the city for several years.

Runaway slaves traveled different routes in their search for freedom. In most instances, the best plan was determined by where the slave lived. This map shows some of the possible routes followed by fugitives. Many of the routes led north to Canada, but others led south toward Mexico and the Caribbean.

Harriet and her group arrived in Philadelphia four days later. They had traveled 100 miles (160 km). The three brothers changed their last names to Stewart for extra protection. William Still helped Harriet arrange the rest of their trip to Canada.

Harriet also boldly led her aging parents to freedom. She traveled to their cabin in 1857, unsure of how she would manage the long journey. She found an old horse and a makeshift cart and seated her parents inside. Knowing how visible they would be, she put her faith, as always, in God.

She headed north just off the main roads to abolitionist Thomas Garrett's home in Wilmington, Delaware. Garrett gave them food, shelter, and money and sent them to William Still. Harriet and her parents made it safely to St. Catharines.

Harriet remained in St. Catharines until her parents were settled with other family members in the community. The former slaves who lived there were happy to be free, but they were extremely poor. Harriet needed money to support her family and friends. She left for Boston to raise money in the abolitionist community.

The Lecture Circuit

Anti-slavery groups wanted to hear Harriet's story about life as a slave, as well as her daring activities as a conductor. Harriet was illiterate, and her sleeping spells occurred often. Yet her memory was remarkable and she had a beautiful, compelling voice. Several speaking engagements helped her gain political support and money for her work.

This display at the National Underground Railroad Freedom Center in Cincinnati, Ohio, shows a wagon with a false bottom. A hidden compartment provided room for runaway slaves who were being transported by abolitionists or other sympathetic supporters.

Thomas Garrett
(1789–1871)

One of Harriet's staunchest friends and supporters during her years as a conductor was Thomas Garrett. Garrett was a Quaker abolitionist and active stationmaster on the Underground Railroad. He made his living as an iron and hardware merchant. Garrett and his family lived in Wilmington, Delaware. Their home was always open to fugitive slaves. Garrett respected Harriet's courage and helped her in any way possible. He provided food and shelter to all who sought refuge. He sometimes gave Harriet money.

Over a period of 40 years, Thomas Garrett helped more than 2,000 slaves on their journey to freedom.

Thomas Garrett, shown here in a photograph taken around 1850, spent most of his young life in Pennsylvania. He moved to the neighboring slave state of Delaware in order to more actively pursue his devotion to the abolitionist cause. There, he openly confronted slave hunters and helped fugitive slaves on the Underground Railroad. He and Harriet Tubman became fast friends as well as colleagues on the Railroad, and today a park in Wilmington is named after both of them.

When Harriet returned to Canada, she realized that life in St. Catharines was too difficult for her parents. She needed a home farther south.

In 1859, U.S. Senator William H. Seward from New York offered Harriet a 7-acre (2.8-hectare) plot of land just outside Auburn. Senator Seward was an opponent of slavery and knew of Harriet's work. The property had a main house as well as outbuildings, enough to accommodate Harriet and other members of her family. The land could be used for farming.

Harriet purchased the property for a low price. She paid the senator in small amounts over a long period of time. She settled her parents and left again to raise funds on the lecture circuit.

Last Trip to Dorchester

In 1860, Harriet made a final trip to Maryland. She was determined to rescue her younger sister Rachel, as well as Rachel's two children. Rachel was the last of Harriet's family remaining on the Brodess property.

When Harriet reached the plantation, she heard Rachel had recently died. The children were somewhere in the region, but out of reach for Harriet. She had to leave them behind. Instead, she took Stephen and Maria Ennals, along with their three children.

The trip was especially long and difficult. The winter was brutally cold, and patrollers were everywhere. Many fearful nights were spent without food or shelter. Harriet's headaches and spells hounded her, but she paid no attention to them. With determination and the help of friends and strangers, she finally managed to relocate the family to Canada.

Over a period of 11 years, Harriet made 13 trips back into slave territory. She personally led about 70 slaves to freedom. She helped at least 50 more by explaining to them how to make their way North.

Harriet's role as a conductor on the Underground Railroad came to an end with the rescue of the Ennals family. She had no idea that she would soon take on another important mission.

CHAPTER FIVE

Nurse, Scout, Spy: The Civil War

In 1860, Abraham Lincoln was elected president of the United States. At that time, several states disagreed on certain issues. Two major points of controversy were the economy and states' rights versus federal control. The northern states were becoming industrialized. Many people worked in factories or other places of business outside their homes. In the South, farming was still the most common way to make a living. Large plantations and some smaller farms relied on slave labor to help bring in crops such as cotton and rice.

As 16th president of the United States, Abraham Lincoln led the country through its most difficult crisis on home territory—the Civil War. His main goal during this time was to maintain the Union. By the end of the war, the United States was still intact, and the existing system of slavery had been abolished as well. President Lincoln was assassinated less than a week after the war ended while attending the theater with his wife. He is considered one of the nation's greatest presidents.

EMANCIPATION

The Gap Widens Between North and South

Economic differences intensified as new territories developed in the western section of the country. The federal government believed new states should be free states. The southern states, which relied heavily on slave labor, believed each new state should have the right to decide whether it would allow slavery or not.

Two years before his election as president, Lincoln had stated:

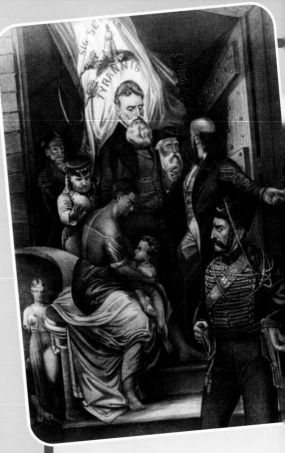

> "A house divided against itself cannot stand. I believe this government cannot endure permanently half-slave and half-free. I do not expect the Union to be dissolved—I do not expect the House to fall—but I do expect it will cease to be divided. It will become all one thing, or all the other."

This 1860 painting by American artist Louis Ransom depicts ardent abolitionist John Brown being led to his execution on December 2, 1859. According to several accounts, Brown, accompanied by guards and officials, paused on the steps to kiss the head of a slave child. At least two other noted artists, Thomas S. Noble ("John Brown's Blessing," 1867) and Thomas Hovenden ("Last Moments of John Brown," 1884) commemorated Brown's final act of kindness through their paintings of this incident.

John Brown (1800–1859)

Harriet Tubman met fierce abolitionist John Brown in the winter of 1858. Brown had heard about Harriet's success as a conductor on the Underground Railroad. He wanted to enlist her help. Brown was recruiting men and weapons for a slave uprising that would bring an end to the bondage of all slaves in the United States.

Harriet was impressed by John Brown and agreed to support his cause. She would help with recruitment and provide any geographical route information that might be of help to him. John Brown referred to Harriet as "General Tubman."

Before meeting Brown in 1858, Harriet began having a recurring dream that confused her until some time later. In the dream, a serpent with the face of an old man wearing a long, white beard lifted its head and looked at her. It seemed the man wanted to speak to her. Two younger serpents came beside him. As Harriet watched in her dream, many men attacked the three serpents, killing the two younger ones first and then the old man.

On Sunday, October 16, 1859, John Brown attacked and secured the military arsenal at Harpers Ferry, Virginia. He and a small group of men, including two of his sons, fought to keep control. His hope was that this rebellion would spark others in the country to take action against a government that supported slavery.

After two days, a group of U.S. Marines forced Brown to retreat. The insurgency was stopped. All but a few of Brown's men were killed or captured. His two sons were killed. John Brown was tried for treason and hanged.

Harriet was in New York when she heard of John Brown's tragic death. She felt great sorrow at the loss of this courageous man who died fighting for the freedom of others. Now she finally understood her dream. The two young serpents were John Brown's sons. The old serpent was John Brown himself. What made her dream even more interesting— and prophetic—was that Brown didn't grow the white beard until he was in jail awaiting his trial and execution!

Following the election, many Southerners were convinced the president would destroy their economy and their way of life. They did not want the federal government to eliminate individual state rights.

Emergence of the Confederacy

A few weeks after Lincoln's election, South Carolina decided to secede, or withdraw from, the Union. Mississippi, Florida, Alabama, Georgia, Louisiana, and Texas soon followed. In early 1861, a total of 11 slave states set up their own nation, the Confederate States of America. The four remaining slave states—Delaware, Kentucky, Maryland, and Missouri—remained with the Union, which now numbered 23 states. They were referred to as "border states." In 1863, a part of Virginia that remained loyal to the Union broke away from Virginia and the rest of the Confederacy and formed a new U.S. state—West Virginia.

The U. S. government did not recognize the Confederacy. President Lincoln wanted to keep the country together. He said that he had no wish to abolish slavery in the states where the system already existed. He wanted to stop slavery from being legal in any new states.

Many slaves who ran away from their masters during the Civil War looked to the Union Army to provide them with food, shelter, and protection. These fugitives were referred to as "contraband." In this illustration, a group of contrabands follow Union General William Tecumseh Sherman as he leads his troops through Georgia.

The War Begins

On April 12, 1861, Confederate soldiers attacked the federal garrison at Fort Sumter in Charleston Harbor, South Carolina. The Civil War, also known as the War Between the States, had begun.

Slaves throughout the South began to flee northward. Many sought refuge at Union military encampments. These fugitives were referred to as "contraband." Union military commanders stationed in the South appealed to the federal government for help.

Harriet and the Military

Massachusetts Governor John Andrew had heard of Harriet Tubman and her ability to lead people out of slavery. He felt that her fearlessness and leadership skills could be of help to the war effort. She could also work as a nurse in contraband hospitals and help gain information from the patients as well as other contrabands about conditions in the South. Andrew asked Harriet to help. Harriet agreed. As she later said, " . . . the good Lord has come down to deliver my people, and I must go and help Him."

A classic image of Harriet Tubman in her Civil War "garb." She is wearing a long skirt or dress, with a coat over the dress. She carries a bag over her right shoulder, wears a bandana over her hair, and carries a long rifle. During the war, Harriet worked as a nurse, scout, and spy for the Union.

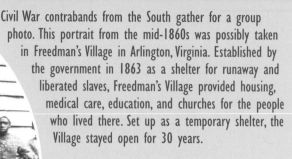

Civil War contrabands from the South gather for a group photo. This portrait from the mid-1860s was possibly taken in Freedman's Village in Arlington, Virginia. Established by the government in 1863 as a shelter for runaway and liberated slaves, Freedman's Village provided housing, medical care, education, and churches for the people who lived there. Set up as a temporary shelter, the Village stayed open for 30 years.

The governor sent Harriet to South Carolina. She would work as a nurse at the makeshift contraband hospitals in the area. She could teach fugitive slaves how to work in the Union military camps. Also, with her experience as a conductor on the Underground Railroad, she could be of service as a scout and spy.

On January 1, 1863, after almost two years of fighting, President Lincoln issued the Emancipation Proclamation. The document stated that all slaves held in states that had seceded from the Union were free. Thousands of slaves were now free, but those in the border states remained in bondage.

After President Lincoln issued the Emancipation Proclamation in 1863, many former slaves joined the Union Army for the remainder of the Civil War. This illustration depicts a freedman fighting to liberate all slaves.

"MAKE WAY FOR LIBERTY!"

Lincoln's intention was to cause a major break in the Confederate forces. The Proclamation also brought the issue of the abolition of slavery to the fore. Former slaves could now enlist in the war. Freed slaves were referred to as "freedmen."

After months of nursing the sick and wounded, Harriet appealed to her military commanders to work more directly behind enemy lines. Using her ability to travel without attracting attention, Harriet began serving as a scout and spy. She moved among the Confederate population, keeping her eyes and ears open. Working as a laundress or cook along the way, Harriet saw firsthand what was happening in the South. She delivered information about troop locations and military plans to Union command.

A Leader, Once Again

In June of 1863, Harriet, accompanied by Union Colonel James Montgomery, led several gunboats of armed black soldiers into enemy territory. Moving up the Combahee River, the group destroyed plantations, railroads, and bridges. They raided warehouses and stockpiles of rebel supplies. Hundreds of slaves ran to the boats, wanting passage to freedom.

A reporter from the Wisconsin State Journal witnessed Harriet's return. In an article about her role in the expedition, he wrote:

> *Col. Montgomery and his gallant band of 300 black soldiers, under the guidance of a black woman, dashed into the enemies' country, struck a bold and effective blow, destroying millions of dollars worth of commissary stores, cotton, and lordly dwellings, and striking terror to the heart of rebellion, brought off nearly 800 slaves and thousands of dollars worth of property, without losing a man or receiving a scratch!*

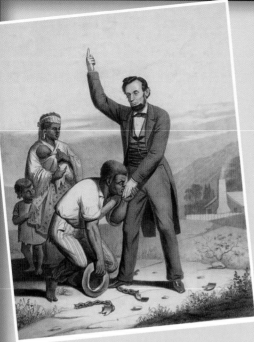

Former slaves who had been freed during and after the Civil War were grateful to President Lincoln for his role in their emancipation. Although the abolition of slavery was not originally a major reason for the conflict, it became a primary focus as the war raged on. Pictures such as this, which showed Lincoln as the great liberator of the slaves, were later criticized as depicting the kneeling slaves in a subordinate role in relation to the tall and upright Lincoln.

The End of Slavery

Following the Combahee expedition, the military granted Harriet a temporary leave. She visited her family in Auburn for a while. She returned to work as a nurse in contraband hospitals, this time in Virginia.

On April 9, 1865, Confederate General Robert E. Lee surrendered to Union General Ulysses S. Grant at Appomattox Courthouse in Virginia.

On April 14, 1865, President Abraham Lincoln was assassinated while attending a theatrical performance with his wife. He had managed to achieve his goal of preserving the Union. In the process, slavery was abolished.

John Wilkes Booth, a stage actor, assassinated President Lincoln. Wilkes shot the president at close range as he sat enjoying a play with his wife and two guests in a private balcony in Ford's Theatre. Although doctors did their best to save his life, President Abraham Lincoln, often referred to as the "Great Emancipator," died nine hours later.

CHAPTER SIX

Aftermath and Legacy

After the war ended, Harriet returned to Auburn. Taking a train back to New York, she was badly injured by a conductor and two other men who physically evicted her from a passenger car because of her race. Harriet arrived home exhausted and in pain from a broken arm and, possibly, several broken ribs.

Shameful Disservice

Harriet's family depended on her for financial support, but she was unable to work for several months because of her injuries, constant headaches, and sleeping spells. She had no available funds. Friends brought food and clothing to her family. They sent a little money when they could. They worried about Harriet's health and the huge responsibility she carried.

In spite of her contributions to the Union and a lifetime of selfless service to others, Harriet always had to worry about finances. She continued to work and support her household until she was very old. This portrait of Harriet, which reflects her strength of character, was taken in Auburn, New York. She was in her 80s at the time.

Lack of money had always been a worry for Harriet. When she did have money, she gave it to others. She petitioned the government on several occasions to receive compensation for her years of work during the war. Never officially a soldier, Harriet was not entitled to a military paycheck or a pension.

Former abolitionist friends as well as military personnel from the war years wrote letters on Harriet's behalf to members of the government. The friends requested back pay for Harriet's years of war service. The letters were sent to politicians who could have remedied the situation, but nothing was resolved. Harriet received no compensation.

New Goals and Challenges

Harriet's home in Auburn was always filled with people. Some were family members. Others were displaced former slaves who needed food or a place to stay. Many former slaves did not know how to support themselves. Harriet never turned anyone away.

To help feed and support the constant stream of people, Harriet farmed the land around her home and planted a huge garden. She sold produce by going door to door in her community. She also rented rooms in her home to a few people who worked in the area.

Harriet's early mission to lead family and friends to freedom had been accomplished. Slavery had been abolished. She and her former abolitionist colleagues faced new challenges. The goals now became equality, freedom of choice, education, and the right to vote.

A Second Marriage

A young man named Nelson Davis was one of Harriet's boarders. Nelson was a veteran of the Civil War. He worked near Harriet's home and rented a room for three years. Nelson was ill with tuberculosis.

Harriet's first husband, John Tubman, had died in 1867. Harriet fell in love with Nelson, who was 20 years younger. The couple married in 1869. A few years later, they adopted a baby girl named Gertie.

Harriet Tubman poses for a photograph with family and friends next to a barn on her property in Auburn c. 1887. Harriet stands at the left of the group. Her husband, Nelson Davis, is seated in a chair wearing a hat, and their adopted daughter Gertie stands between them.

Nelson and Harriet opened a brick-making business on Harriet's property. Nelson probably did not work regularly because of his illness. Financial difficulties continued to be a part of Harriet's life. Her home was still open to those in need. She and Nelson took in boarders, and Harriet often worked as a domestic.

Mrs. Bradford's Book and a Personal Loss

Sarah H. Bradford, a schoolteacher and neighbor, wanted to help Harriet. In 1868, Mrs. Bradford had several conversations with Harriet about her past experiences. She also contacted many of Harriet's friends and associates, asking them for stories about Harriet's life and work. Mrs. Bradford's biography of Harriet, titled Scenes in the Life of Harriet Tubman, was published in 1869. All proceeds went to Harriet. With the profits, Harriet was able to pay some of her debts and worry a little less about money for a while.

Harriet slowed down a little as the years went by, but she remained an active member of her community. She continued to help former slaves make better lives for themselves. She shared all she had with those less fortunate.

Nelson Davis died in 1888. A few years later, Harriet began to receive a small pension from the government. She never received compensation for her own service. This pension was awarded to Harriet as a war veteran's widow.

Back in the Public Eye

In her late 60s, Harriet decided to reenter the public arena. She wanted to take on a more active role for women's rights. She became a member of the National American Woman Suffrage Association (NAWSA). This group included prominent suffragists Susan B. Anthony, Elizabeth Cady Stanton, and Emily Howland among its members. For several years, Harriet attended meetings and conventions in Boston, New York, and Washington, D.C. She was often a featured speaker. At one convention in 1896, at age 74, Harriet said of her experiences as conductor on the Underground Railroad, ". . . I can say what most conductors can't say—I never ran my train off the track, and I never lost a passenger."

Also in 1896, Harriet bought 25 acres (10 ha) of land next to her home in Auburn. She wanted to build a new home for poor, homeless, and aged African Americans. She had no money, but the bank still granted her a loan for the property. Harriet made payments from the work she still managed. Local civic groups collected money through

Harriet's courage and leadership in the fight for liberty and equality made her a living legend. By the latter part of her life, many people in the United States and foreign countries had heard of her remarkable spirit and accomplishments. Tributes to the memory of Harriet's vision escalated after her death and continue today. This photograph, probably the last taken of Harriet, dates to 1912. Harriet, seated in a wheelchair, was about 90 years old at the time.

Commemorating Harriet

Unable to read or write, Harriet Tubman strongly supported quality education for everyone. Many schools around the country are named after her. In 1944, The U.S. Maritime commission launched the S.S. *Harriet Tubman*, which was one of a group of hundreds of cargo ships, known as Liberty ships, built to carry supplies to Europe. This was the first Liberty ship named after an African-American woman. On February 1, 1978, the U.S. Postal Service issued the Harriet Ross Tubman stamp—again, the first to honor an African-American woman. A second Harriet Tubman stamp, part of a Civil War series, was issued in 1995. In 1990, President George H.W. Bush officially designated March 10 as Harriet Tubman Day. Many books have been written about her colorful, incredible life.

fundraisers. People around the world also had heard of Harriet. Many sent financial contributions to her cause.

Final Mission Accomplished

In 1903, Harriet donated the property to the African Methodist Episcopal Zion Church of Auburn. The Harriet Tubman Home for the Aged opened in 1908.

Harriet entered the Harriet Tubman Home in 1911 and remained there until her death on March 10, 1913. According to many people, her last words to those who held vigil at her bedside were, "I go to prepare a place for you." Harriet was 91 years old.

Harriet Tubman Home

The Harriet Tubman Home in Auburn, New York, was Harriet's dream for poor, aged African Americans. Built on property she donated to her church, Harriet lived to see the home built. She died there in 1913. The home began to falter after Harriet's death. It was finally closed and abandoned for almost 20 years. The AME Zion Church eventually organized a major fund drive. The restored Harriet Tubman Home was dedicated in 1953. Today, the home is a museum and education center that honors Harriet's enduring legacy.

Hundreds of people attended Harriet's service at AME Zion Church. She was given a military burial at Fort Hill Cemetery in Auburn. One year later, a bronze plaque with Harriet's image and a small list of her accomplishments was unveiled at a special ceremony. Dr. Booker T. Washington, president of Tuskegee Institute in Alabama, was guest speaker at this memorial celebration. He spoke about Harriet as a heroic role model for people of all races and spanning all generations. Today, the bronze plaque is attached to the Cayuga County Courthouse building in Auburn.

A Tribute to a Heroine

The headstone at Harriet's grave in Fort Hill Cemetery in Auburn, New York, bears the following epitaph:

**To the Memory of
HARRIET TUBMAN DAVIS**
Heroine of the Underground Railroad
Nurse and Scout in the Civil War
Born about 1820 in Maryland
Died March 10, 1913,
at Auburn, New York
"Servant of God, Well Done"

Rosa Parks (1913–2005)

In 1913, the year of Harriet Tubman's death, a baby girl named Rosa Louise McCauley was born in Tuskegee, Alabama. In 1955, that girl, now grown-up, married, working as a seamstress, and named Rosa Parks, made a brave decision to declare her fight against racial inequality. On December 1, Rosa was riding home from work on a public bus in Montgomery, Alabama. When the bus filled, the driver told Rosa to give up her seat for a white person. She refused and was arrested. Rosa's quiet call to arms resulted in a 13-month boycott against the Montgomery Bus System. Her action also brought new life to the ongoing struggle for civil rights in the country. Backed by the NAACP (National Association for the Advancement of Colored People) and the efforts of emerging African American leader Martin Luther King, Jr., Rosa's case went to the Supreme Court. The Montgomery Bus System was ordered to accept and enforce integration.

After years of being forced to sit in back of buses and giving up her seat to white passengers, Rosa Parks quietly but firmly protested this inequality. Here, Rosa (center in dark coat and hat), a courageous American civil rights activist, rides in a seat of her choice with fellow passengers following the Montgomery, Alabama, bus boycott in 1956.

A Lasting Legacy

Harriet's life struggle to achieve freedom, equality, and opportunity for herself and others influenced succeeding generations of African Americans. Regarded as an early icon of civil rights, Harriet served as an inspiration for leaders and supporters of the modern American Civil Rights Movement of the 1950s and 1960s. Courageous African Americans such as Rosa Parks, John Lewis, and Martin Luther King, Jr., among many others, echoed Harriet's cry for equality from more than a century earlier.

Harriet Tubman lived a remarkable and heroic life—as a slave, abolitionist, nurse, scout, spy, family caretaker, humanitarian, activist, and free woman of faith and character. Her life story stands as a shining reminder of what anyone can accomplish against all odds.

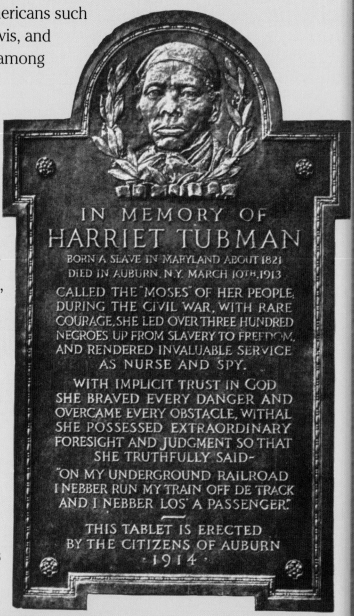

IN MEMORY OF
HARRIET TUBMAN
BORN A SLAVE IN MARYLAND ABOUT 1821
DIED IN AUBURN, N.Y. MARCH 10TH, 1913

CALLED THE "MOSES" OF HER PEOPLE
DURING THE CIVIL WAR, WITH RARE
COURAGE, SHE LED OVER THREE HUNDRED
NEGROES UP FROM SLAVERY TO FREEDOM,
AND RENDERED INVALUABLE SERVICE
AS NURSE AND SPY.

WITH IMPLICIT TRUST IN GOD
SHE BRAVED EVERY DANGER AND
OVERCAME EVERY OBSTACLE, WITHAL
SHE POSSESSED EXTRAORDINARY
FORESIGHT AND JUDGMENT SO THAT
SHE TRUTHFULLY SAID—

"ON MY UNDERGROUND RAILROAD
I NEBBER RUN MY TRAIN OFF DE TRACK
AND I NEBBER LOS' A PASSENGER."

THIS TABLET IS ERECTED
BY THE CITIZENS OF AUBURN
·1914·

The bronze plaque unveiled at a special memorial service for Harriet a year after her death bears witness to the tremendous impact of her courage, faith, and vision.

c. 1822 Araminta "Minty" Ross is born a slave on a plantation in Dorchester County, Maryland. She later changes her name to Harriet.

1828 Harriet is hired out for the first time to the James Cook family by her master, Edward Brodess. Over the next several years, she works for many other masters.

c. 1834 Harriet is hit in the head by a two-pound weight. She survives but suffers serious consequences from the injury for the rest of her life.

1836 Harriet is hired out to John T. Stewart. The Stewart family owns a farm, general store, lumber business, and shipyard.

1844 Harriet marries John Tubman, a free black man.

1849 Harriet escapes to freedom. With the help of strangers on the Underground Railroad, faith in God, and personal courage, she makes her way to Philadelphia, Pennsylvania.

1850 The Fugitive Slave Law is passed in the United States. The law strengthens other legislation requiring that all runaway slaves be returned to their owners. Harriet becomes a conductor on the Underground Railroad. Her first mission is to arrange the rescue of her niece Kessiah and Kessiah's two children.

1851 Harriet helps in the rescue of her brother Moses. She returns to Dorchester County, Maryland, to convince her husband, John, to join her in Philadelphia. John has remarried and does not leave with Harriet.

1854 Harriet successfully leads her brothers Robert, Ben, and Henry to freedom. Her reputation as a fearless conductor grows.

1857 Harriet leads her aging parents to freedom and safety.

1859 Harriet moves her parents and other family members to a new home in Auburn, New York.

1860 Harriet makes a final trip as a conductor to rescue her sister Rachel and Rachel's two children. Harriet learns that Rachel has died and her children are out of reach. Harriet then leads the Stephen Ennals family to freedom. Abraham Lincoln is elected president of the United States.

1861 The Civil War begins on April 12 with an attack on Fort Sumter in Charleston Harbor, South Carolina.

1861–1865 Harriet works as a nurse, scout, and spy in the Civil War.

1863 Harriet leads an armed military expedition with Union Colonel James Montgomery along the Combahee River. Several gunboats of soldiers destroy enemy property, free slaves, and confiscate crops, provisions, and military supplies.

1865 The Civil War ends on April 9 with the surrender of Confederate General Robert E. Lee at Appomattox Court House in Virginia.

1865 President Abraham Lincoln is assassinated on April 14.

1867 John Tubman dies.

1868 Sarah H. Bradford writes a biography of Harriet titled *Scenes in the Life of Harriet Tubman*. All profits go to Harriet.

1869 Harriet marries Nelson Davis, a Civil War veteran.

1888 Nelson Davis dies of tuberculosis.

1890s Harriet becomes actively involved in the suffragist movement.

1896 Harriet purchases 25 acres of land next to her residence in Auburn, New York. Her purpose is to build a home for homeless and aged African Americans.

1903 Harriet donates the 25 acres of land to the African Methodist Episcopal (A.M.E. Zion Church of Auburn.

1908 The Harriet Tubman Home officially opens.

1913 Harriet Tubman dies on March 10. She is buried in Fort Hill Cemetery in Auburn.

abolitionist A person who supports the end of slavery.

bondage The state of being a slave or servant.

controversial Causing disagreement or argument.

docile Obedient; easy to manage.

domestic (n) A housekeeper or servant in another's home.

economy The system of using money and resources in an organization, state, or country.

elude To avoid or escape.

evict To force out; to eject.

federal Relating to a nation's central government.

fugitive A person who runs away or escapes.

garrison A military fort or post.

gourd A fruit with a hard rind. Gourds can be scooped of their fruit and used as containers or utensils.

harbor (v) To provide shelter or a safe place.

icon A symbol or emblem.

integration The uniting or blending of different groups (such as races) to an equal level in society.

manumit To release from slavery.

maternal Relating to a mother's family or ancestry.

overseer A supervisor or manager.

patrollers In the days of American slavery, people who moved about the countryside in search of runaway slaves.

pension Money paid as a reward or acknowledgment for years of service.

plantation A very large farm or agricultural estate that usually requires many laborers to live on the property.

prophetic Relating to predictions or having an ability to see the future.

refuge A safe place; shelter.

secede To withdraw, or break away, from a group or organization.

seizure A sudden attack, such as a loss of consciousness, that results from a disturbance in brain patterns.

sibling A brother or sister.

spiritual (n) A deeply emotional religious song.

stationmaster On the Underground Railroad, a person who offered his or her home as a haven for runaway slaves.

suffragist Anyone who supports the right of women to vote.

terrain An area of land; ground.

tuberculosis A contagious disease that affects the lungs.

Union The United States of America, as a national entity, especially during the period of the Civil War.

Books

Allen, Thomas B. Harriet Tubman, Secret Agent: How Daring Slaves and Free Blacks Spied for the Union During the Civil War. National Geographic, 2006.

Editors of Time for Kids with Renee Skelton. Time for Kids: Harriet Tubman: A Woman of Courage. HarperCollins, 2005.

Hamilton, Virginia. Many Thousands Gone: African Americans from Slavery to Freedom. Knopf Books for Young Readers, 2002.

Hudson, Wade. The Underground Railroad (Cornerstones of Freedom). Children's Press, 2007.

DVD

Freeman, Morgan (narrator). Follow the Drinking Gourd: A Story of the Underground Railroad. American Legends and Heroes series. Rabbit Ears Press & Co., 1994.

Web Sites

www.pbs.org/wgbh/aia/home.html
A PBS site that includes information presented in a four-part series on the African slavery experience in America. Each era includes a historical narrative, relevant images, documents, stories, biographies, and commentaries. The section devoted specifically to Tubman on this site is: www.pbs.org/wgbh/aia/part4/4p1535.html.

www.americaslibrary.gov/cgi-bin/page.cgi/aa/tubman
Information about Harriet Tubman from the Library of Congress. Through photos and written descriptions, this site section on Tubman focuses on four short segments: a basic biography, Harriet's flight to freedom, her role as a conductor for the Underground Railroad, and her activities as a spy in the Civil War.

www.harriettubmanbiography.com/
Web base for biographer Kate Clifford Larson's book on Harriet Tubman. Offers photos and valuable information on the various stages and events in Tubman's life. The site is easy to navigate.

www.harriettubman.com/index.html
Interesting site that provides valuable facts and photos relating to Harriet Tubman's life, times, and mission. A varied collection of information on significant figures in Tubman's life, as well as memorials, historical documents, and activities. Includes current videos and information on U.S. events and people who champion Tubman's causes.

www.nationalgeographic.com/railroad/j1.html
Educational and eye-opening interactive presentation highlighting the work of the Underground Railroad. Visitors are encouraged to learn more about the Underground RR by taking the journey themselves. This creative site also offers Faces of Freedom, Timelines, Possible Routes, a fun "Did You Know?" section, and more.

www.galenfrysinger.com/underground_railroad_museum.htm
A beautiful look inside this center in Cincinnati, Ohio. Visitors to the site can see the museum structure, obtain information relating to the U.S. slave trade, and learn about the role of the Underground Railroad in the fight to abolish slavery. Stunning close-ups of exhibits and artwork make this site a "must-see."

Index

About the Author

Patricia Lantier has written more than 30 books for children. A former educator and publishing executive, she is currently a freelance writer and editor. She earned a B.A. and M.A. from the University of Louisiana-Lafayette and a Ph.D. in English from Marquette University in Milwaukee. In addition to writing, she spends time creating jewelry, gardening, cooking Cajun food, and traveling. She lives in the beautiful Wisconsin countryside on several unspoiled acres of land with her husband Michael, an amazing array of wildlife, and a spectacular view of the night sky.